Becoming a Frog

Greg Roza

Rosen Classroom Books & Materials™
New York

Frogs go through a **metamorphosis** as they become adults.

Most frogs begin life as tiny
eggs. These eggs change into
tadpoles. Tadpoles live in water.

Tadpoles have **gills**. They use their gills to breathe in water.

Tadpoles have tails for swimming.

As tadpoles change, they develop a head. They also develop a long tongue for eating bugs.

Tadpoles grow back legs and front legs. Tadpoles lose their tails as they grow.

Tadpoles develop **lungs** and can breathe air. Their gills disappear beneath their skin.

When the tadpoles have legs and
lungs, they are frogs.

Frogs have strong legs that help them jump.

Frogs will produce eggs that will hatch into new tadpoles.

Glossary

gills — Slits on the sides of an animal that allow it to breathe in water.

lungs — Body parts inside an animal that allow it to breathe air.

metamorphosis — A series of changes that certain animals go through as they grow from eggs to adults.

tadpoles — Young frogs in their first stage of development.